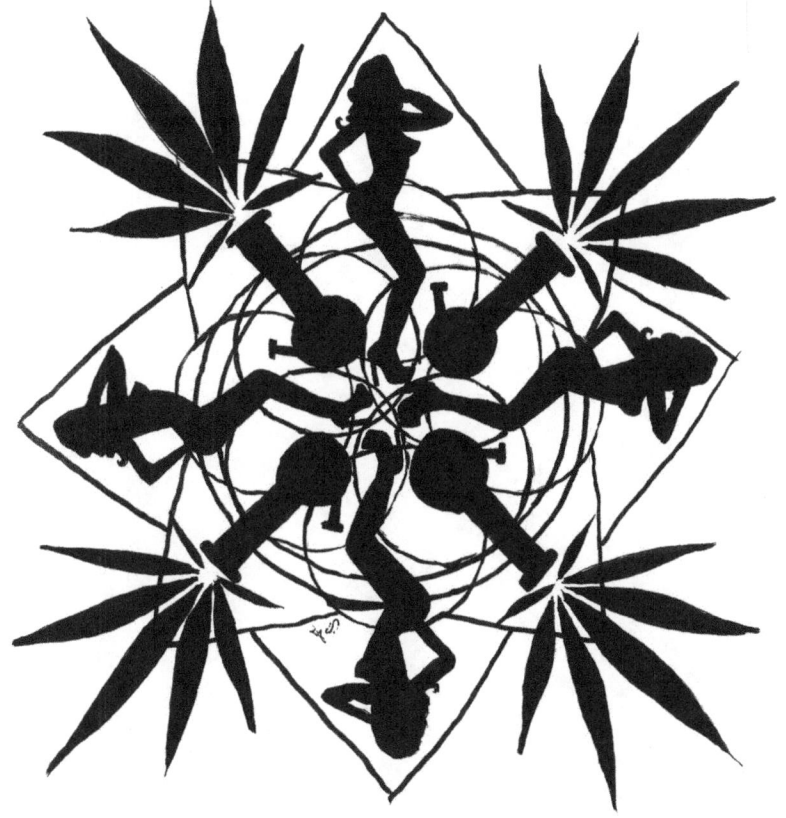

Kush Color

Thank you to all the growers who grew the weed
that inspired the drawings in this coloring book.
Thank you to TLPC_LA for the hours of doodle time,
all wonderful people, new friends, the ideas,
the joints, the munchie foods
without you guys this would have never happened.

And Thank you/ hello to all of you who are buying or
just receiving this coloring book thank you so much for the support!!!!!
We can't wait to see what you do and how you make it your own.
Enjoy Get baked make your self a snack and get to coloring

SAP & KN

on instagram @superapplepie #kushcolor

For best results use crayons or colored pencils, markers will bleed.

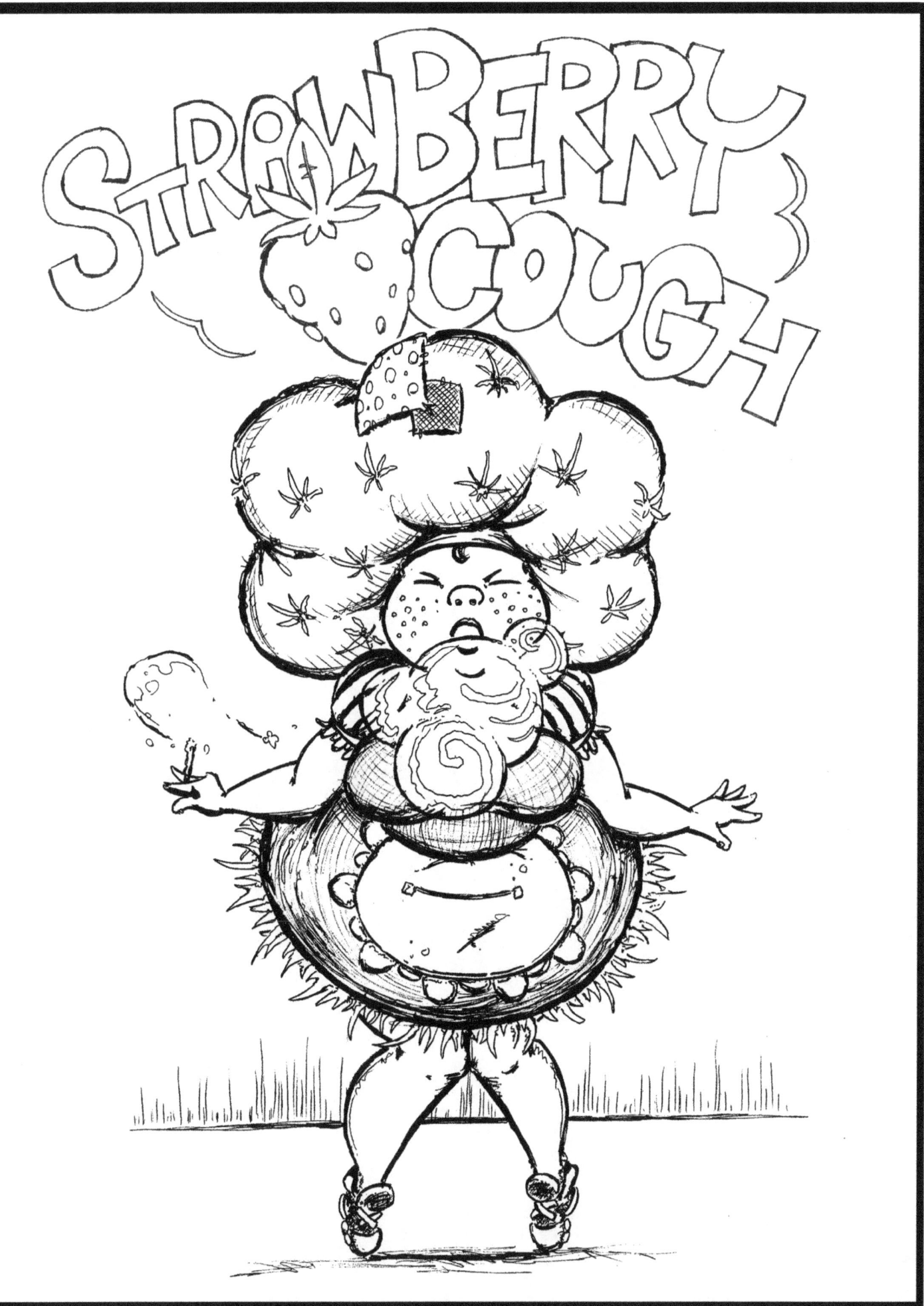

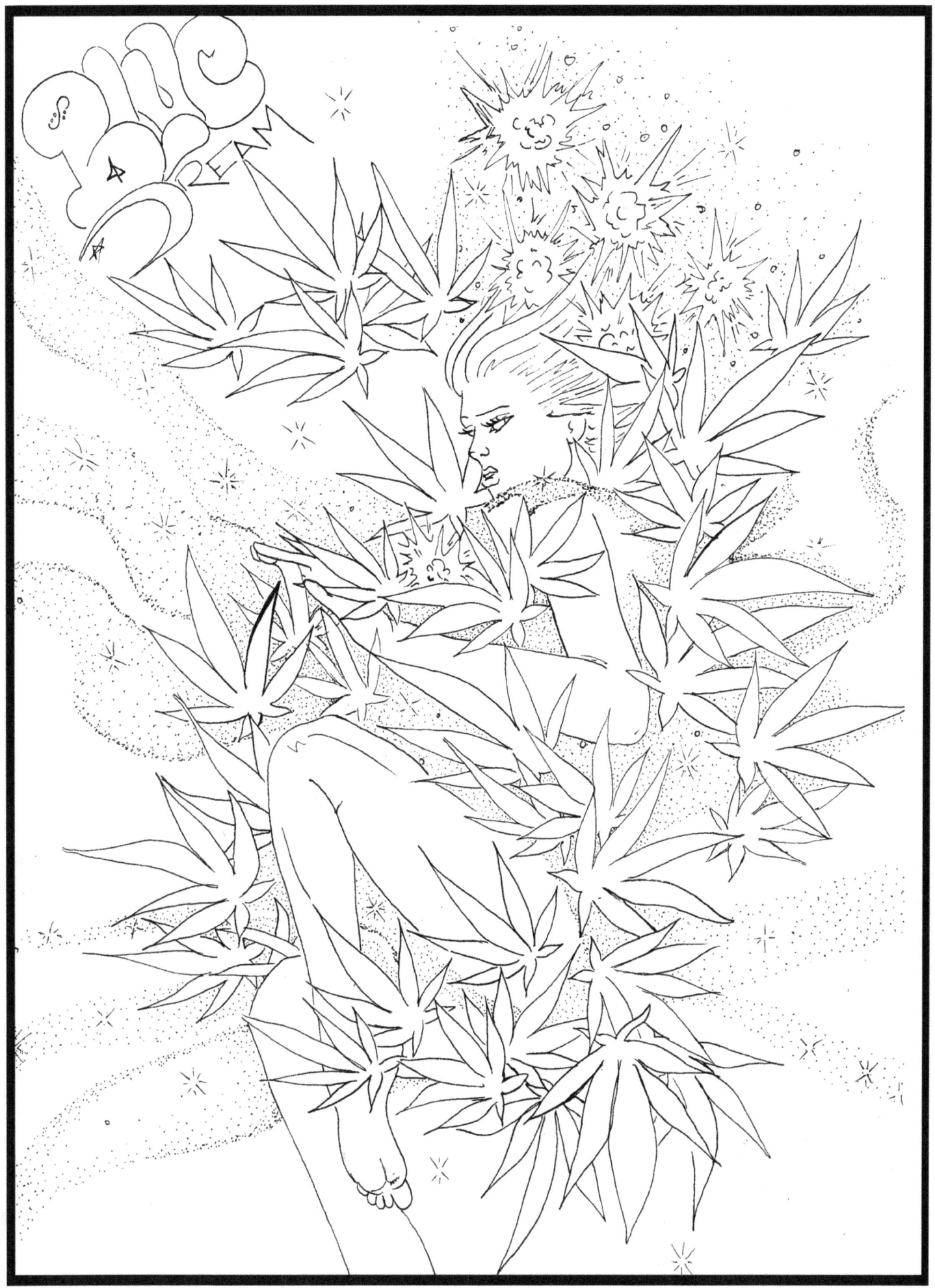

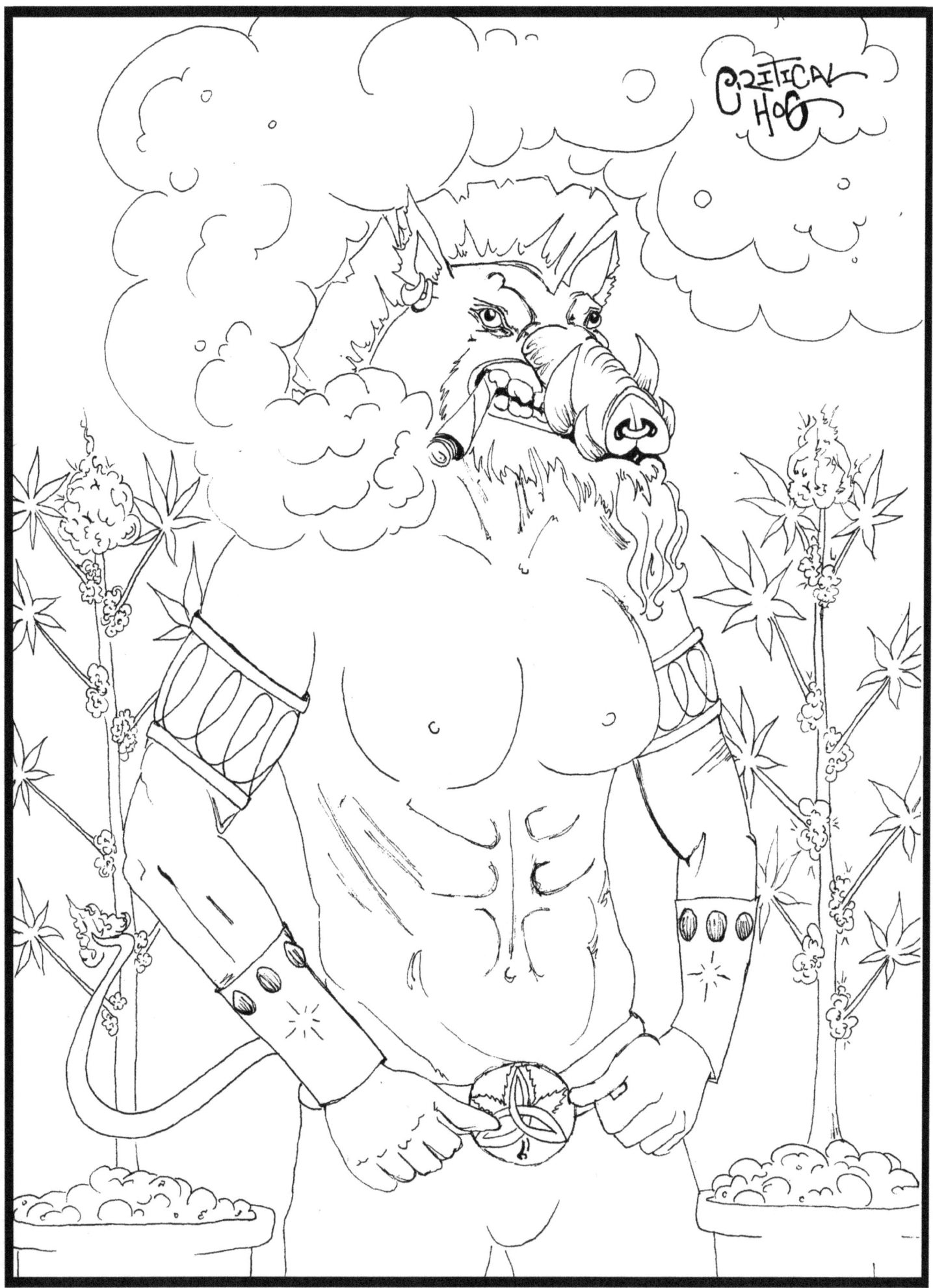

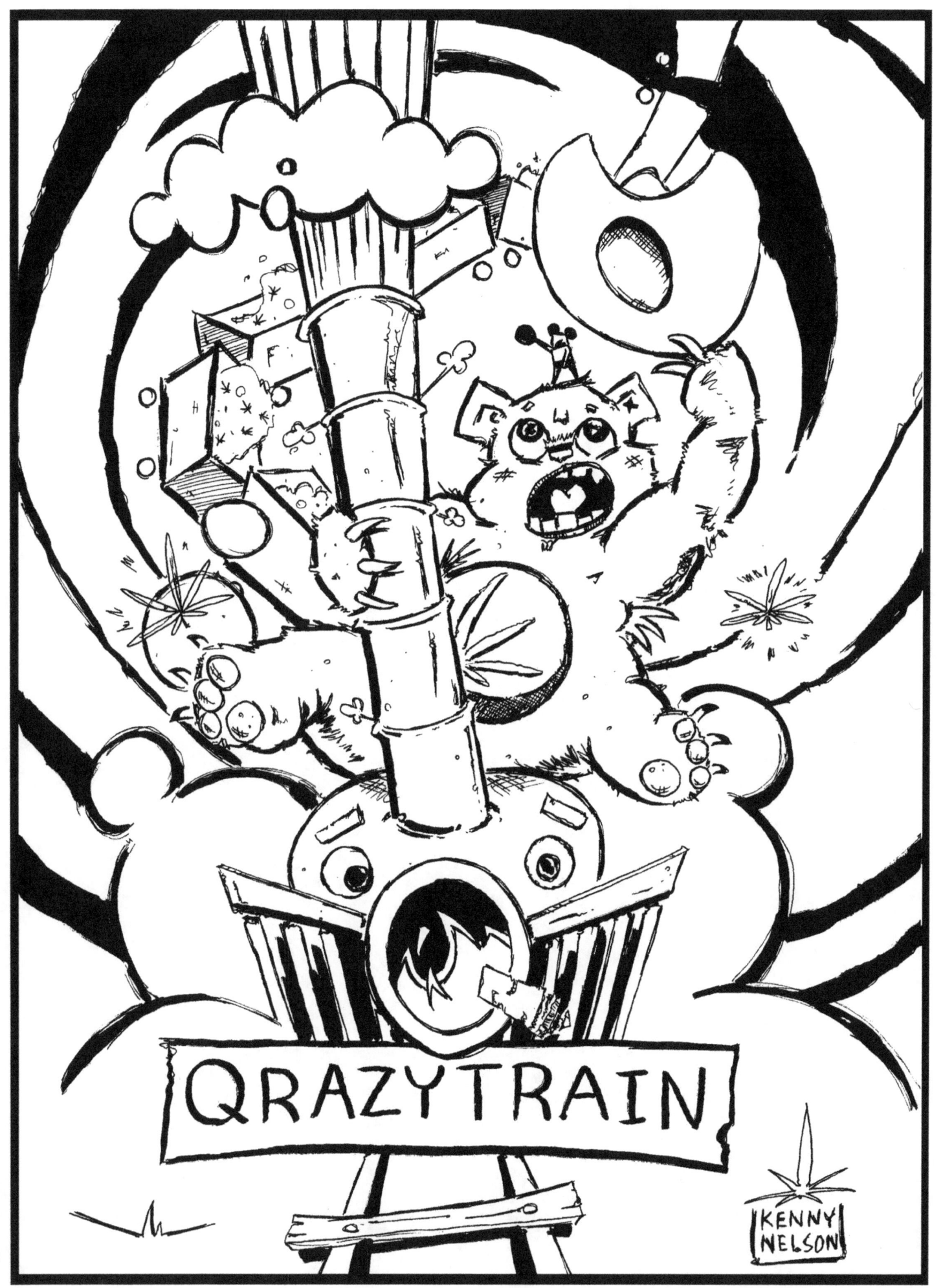

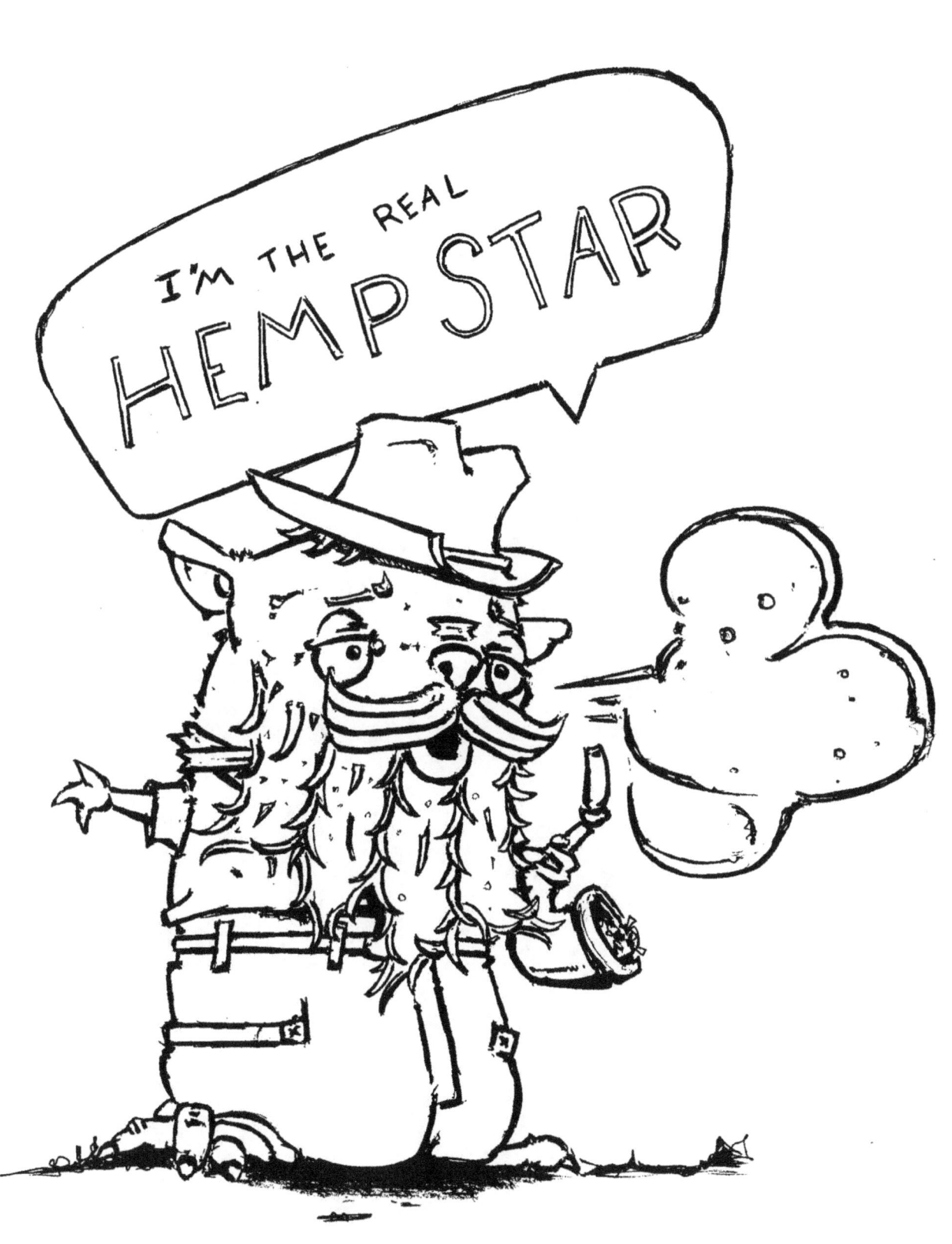

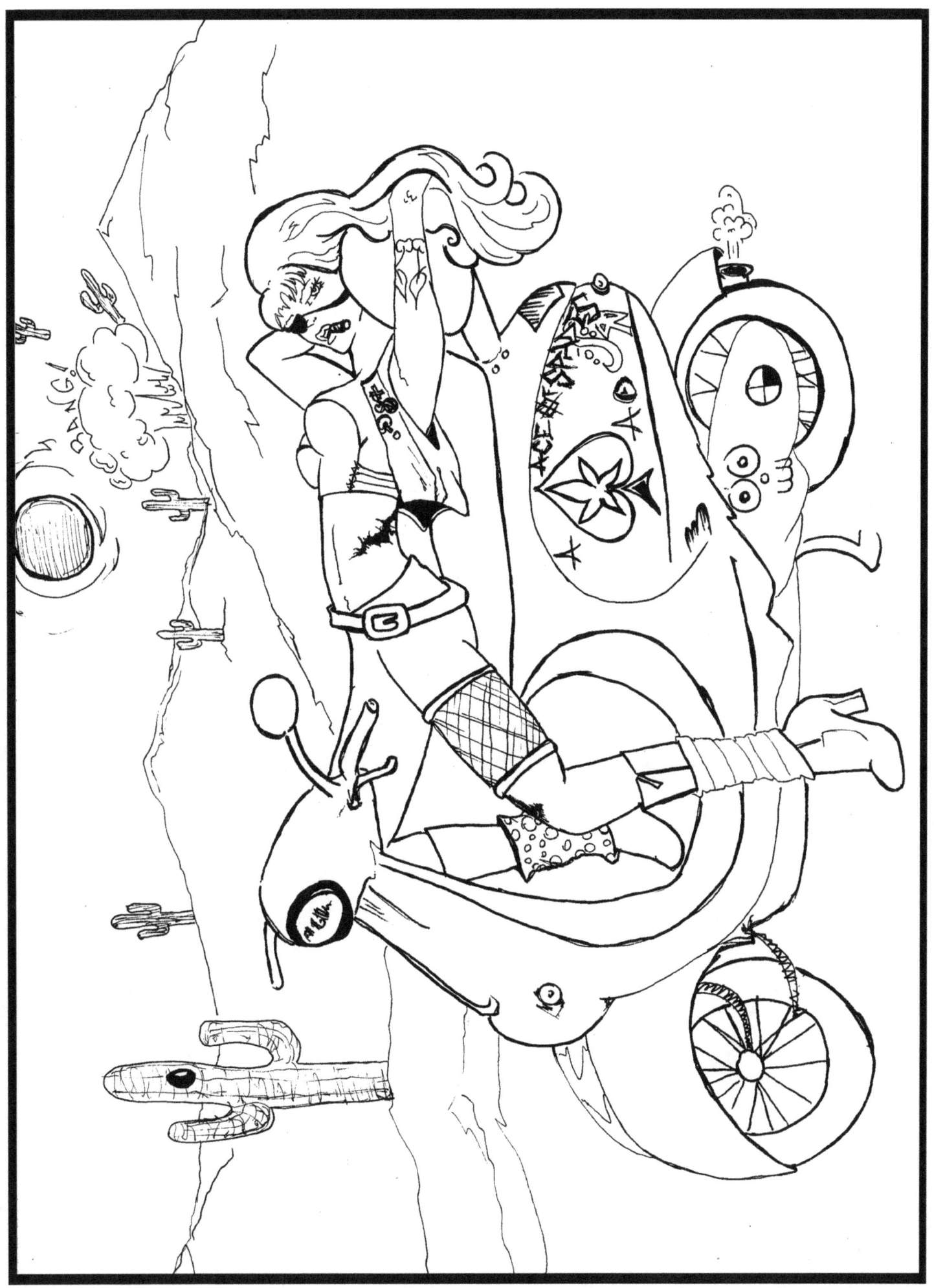

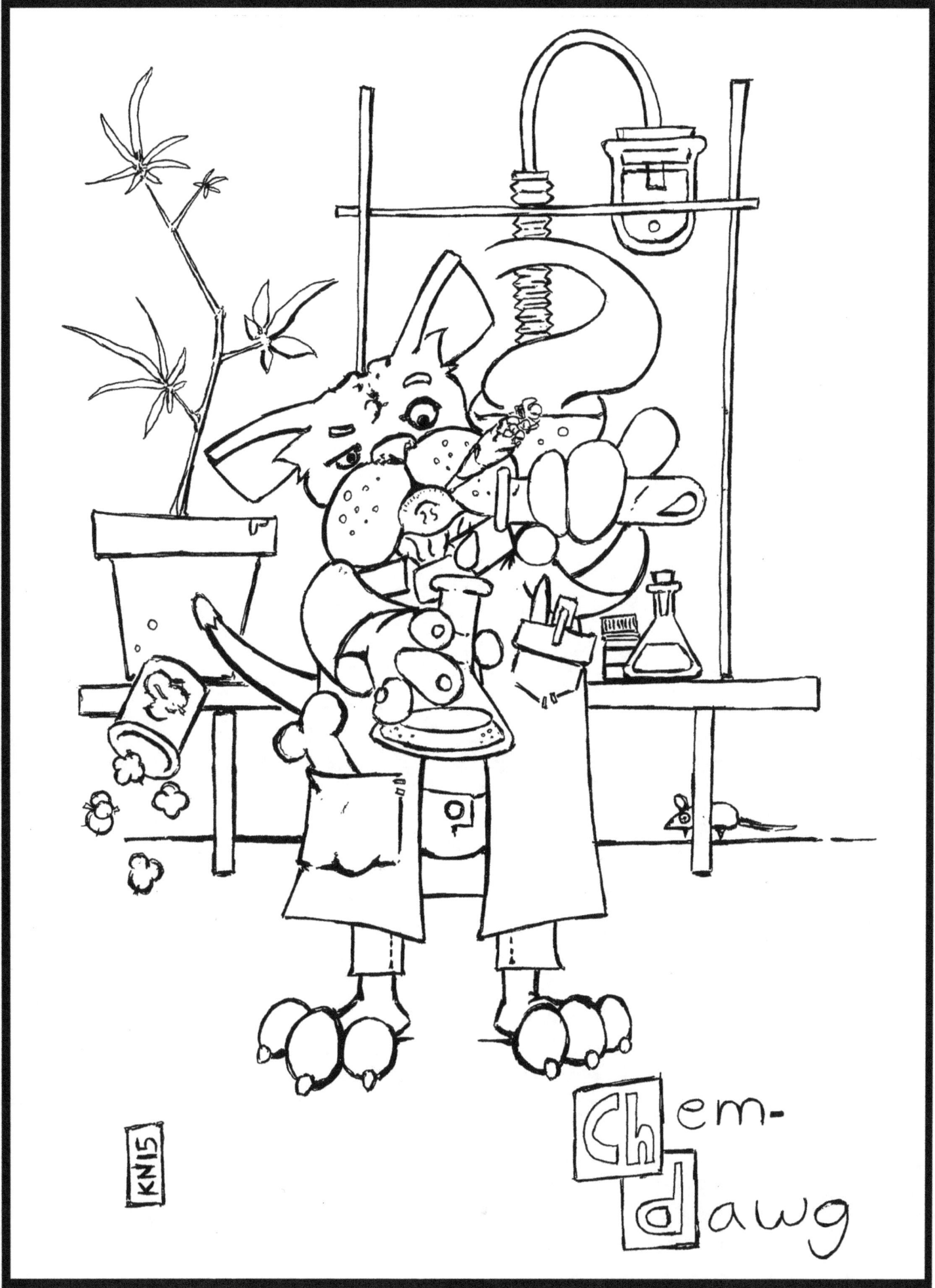

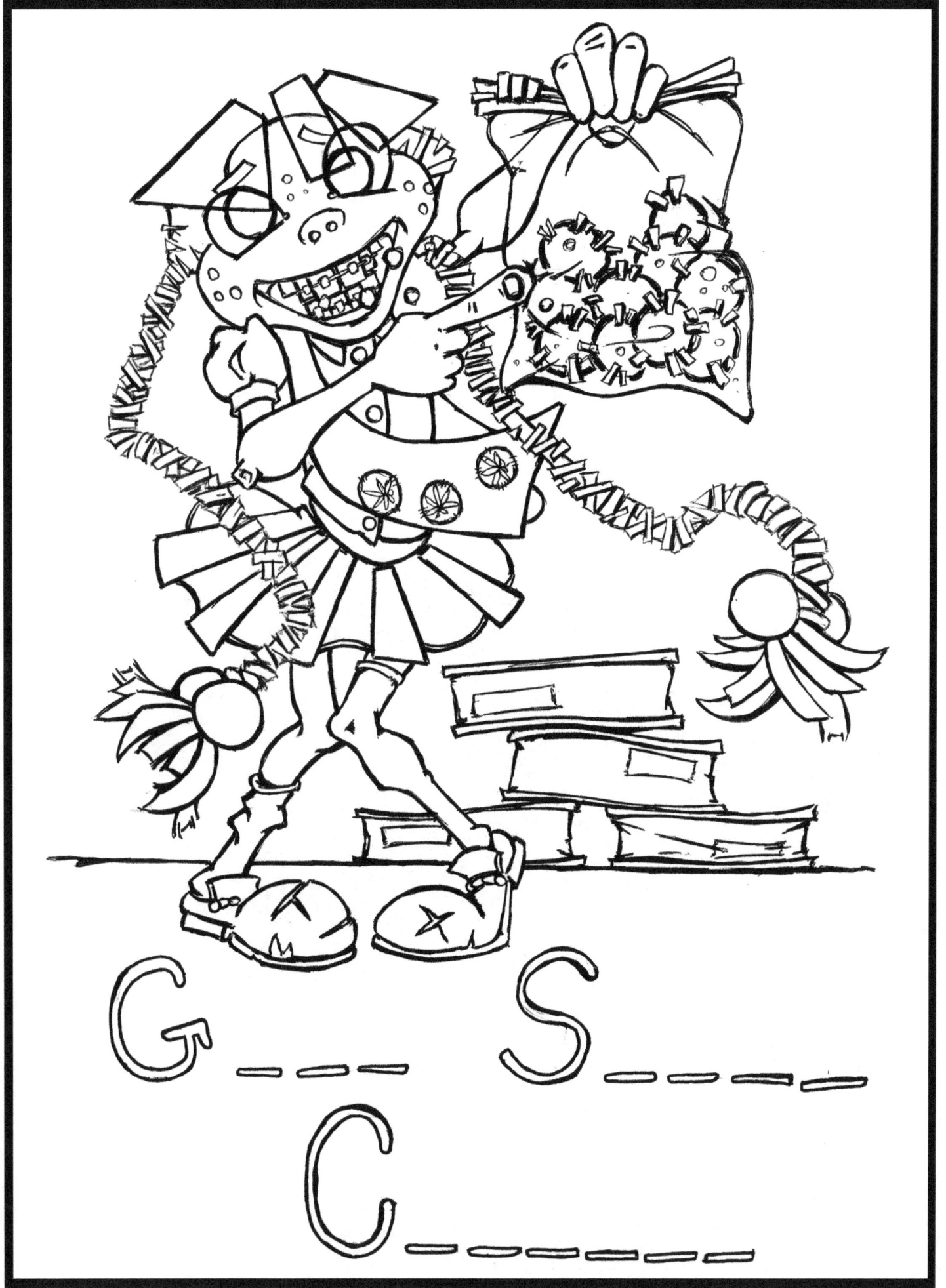

G _ _ _ _   S _ _ _ _ _

C _ _ _ _ _ _ _ _

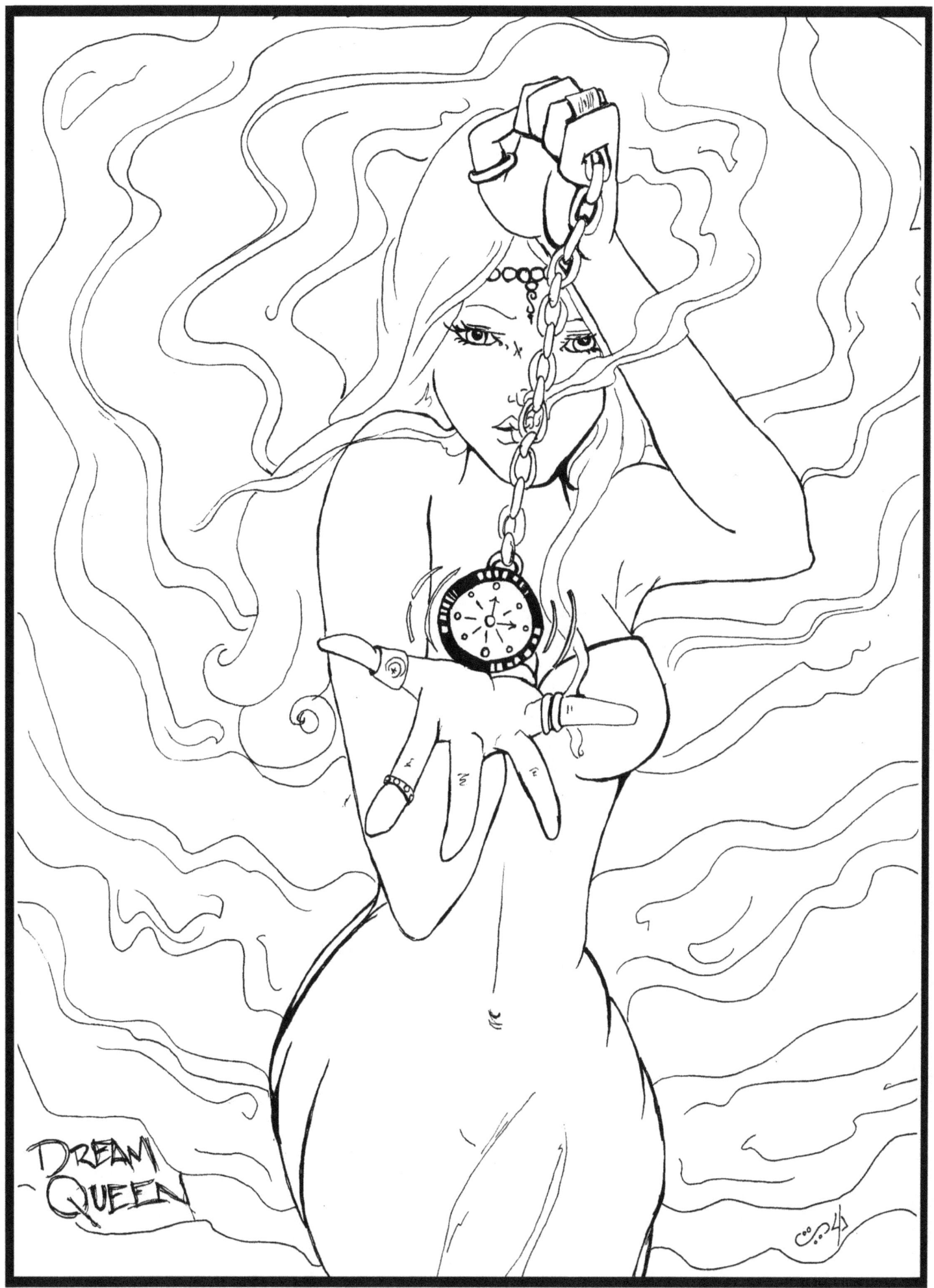

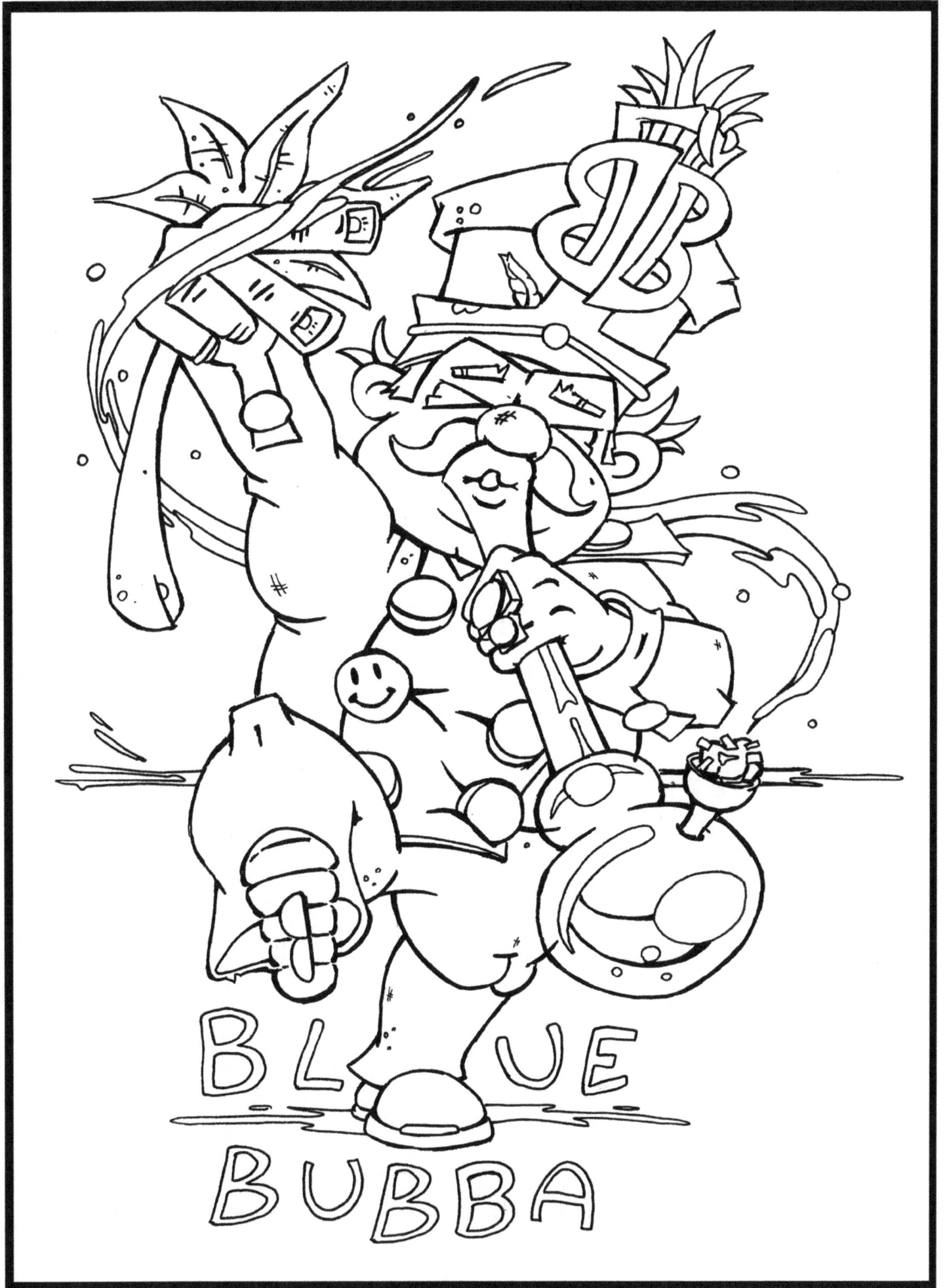

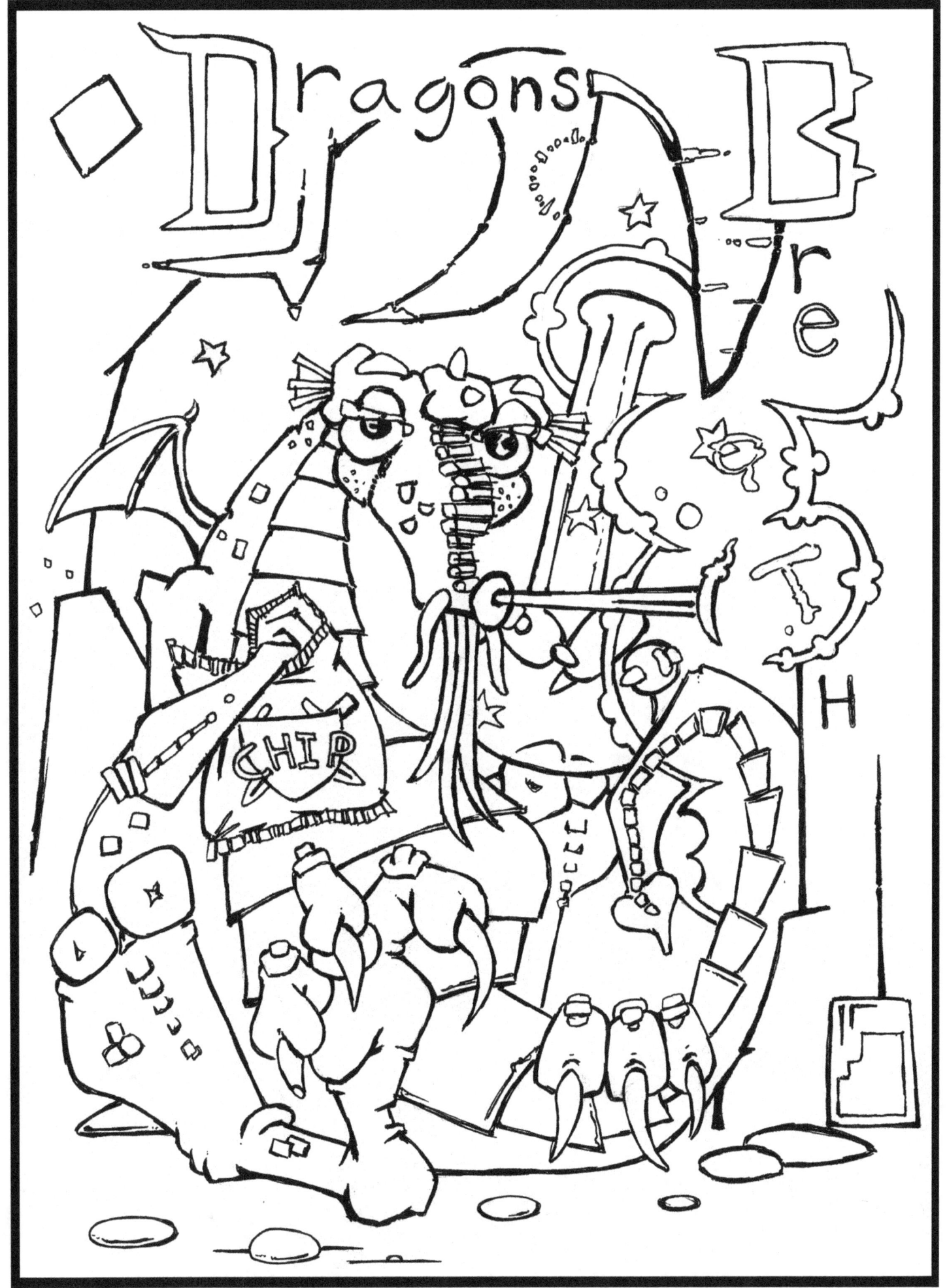

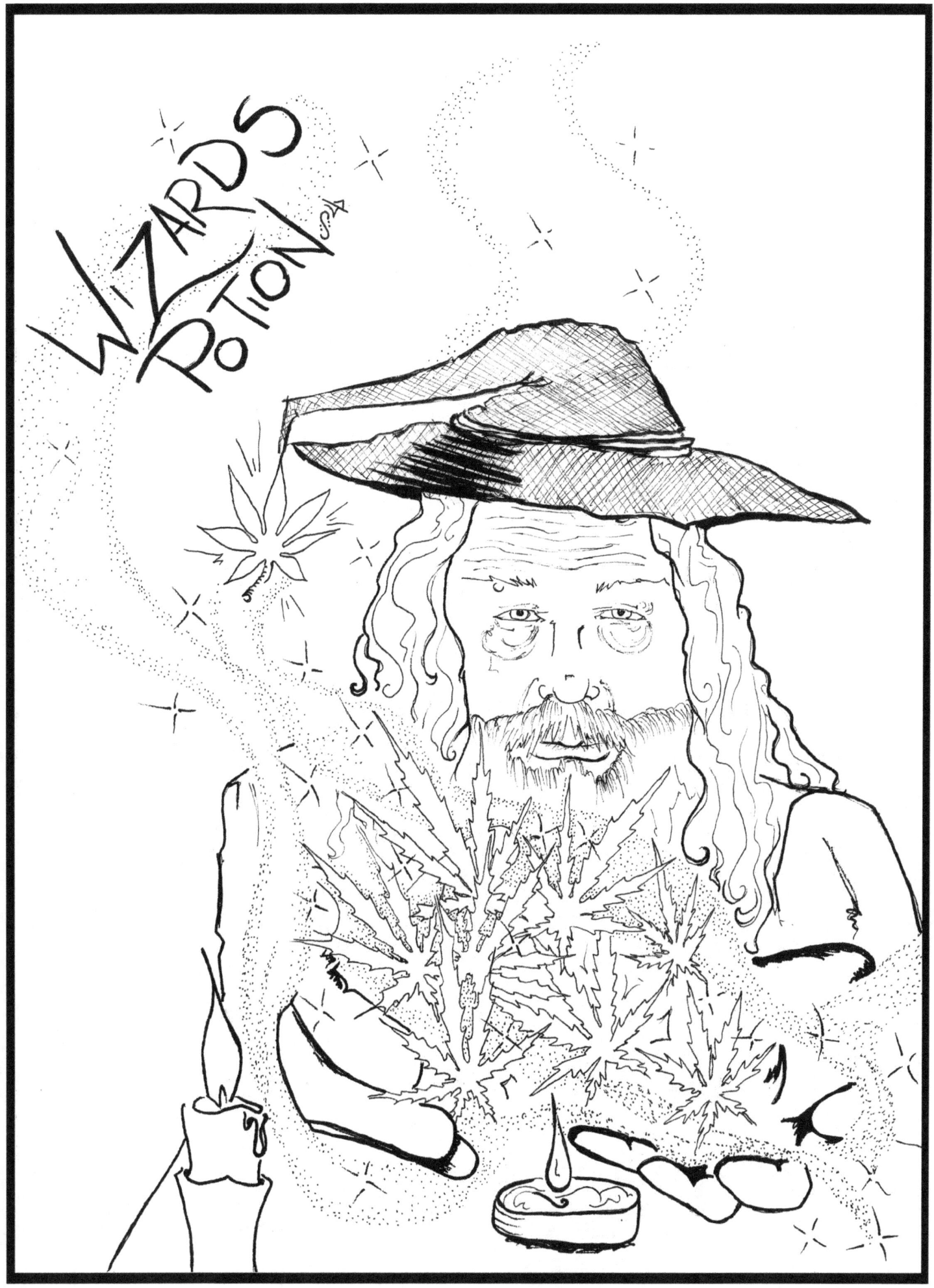

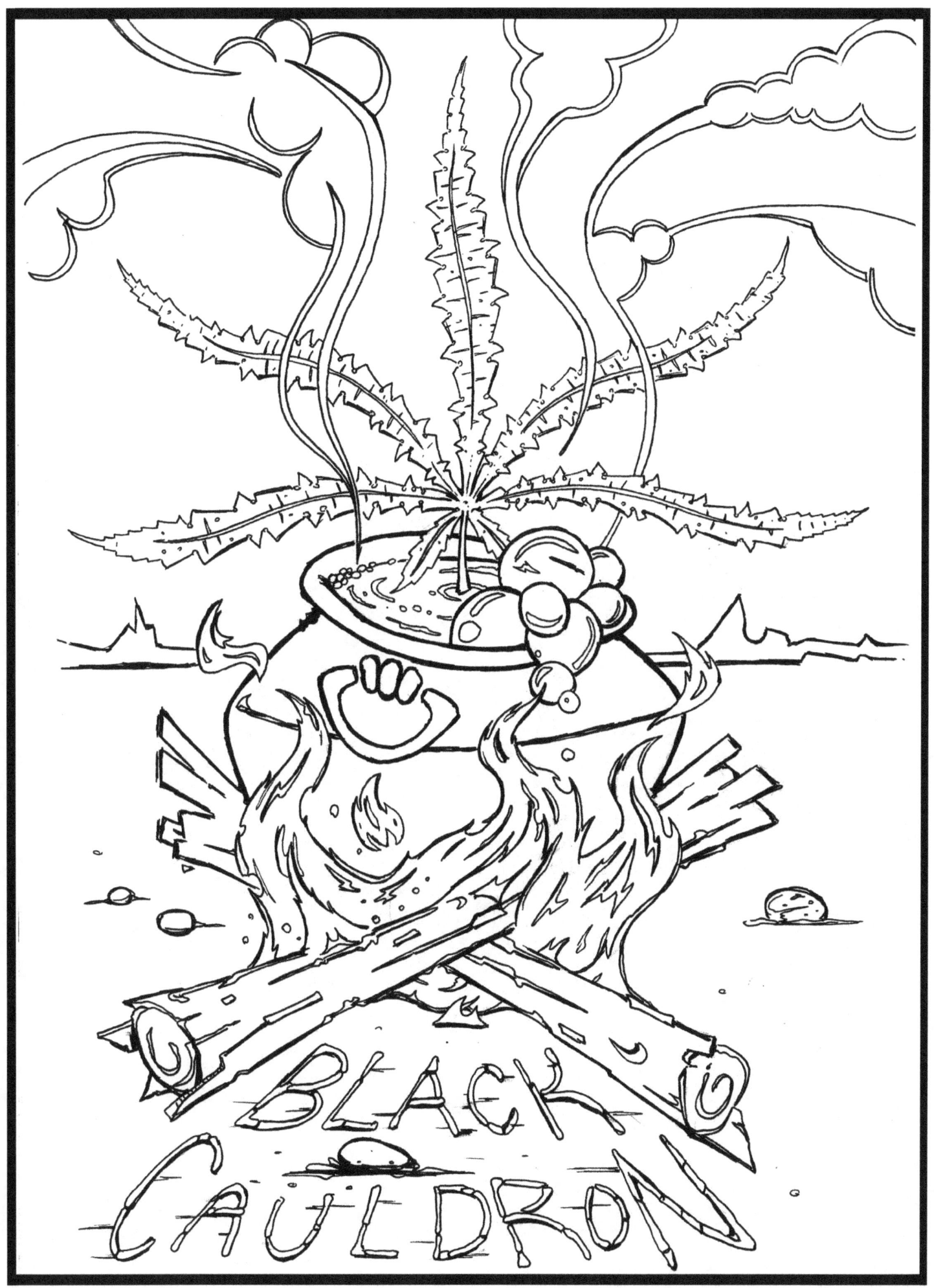

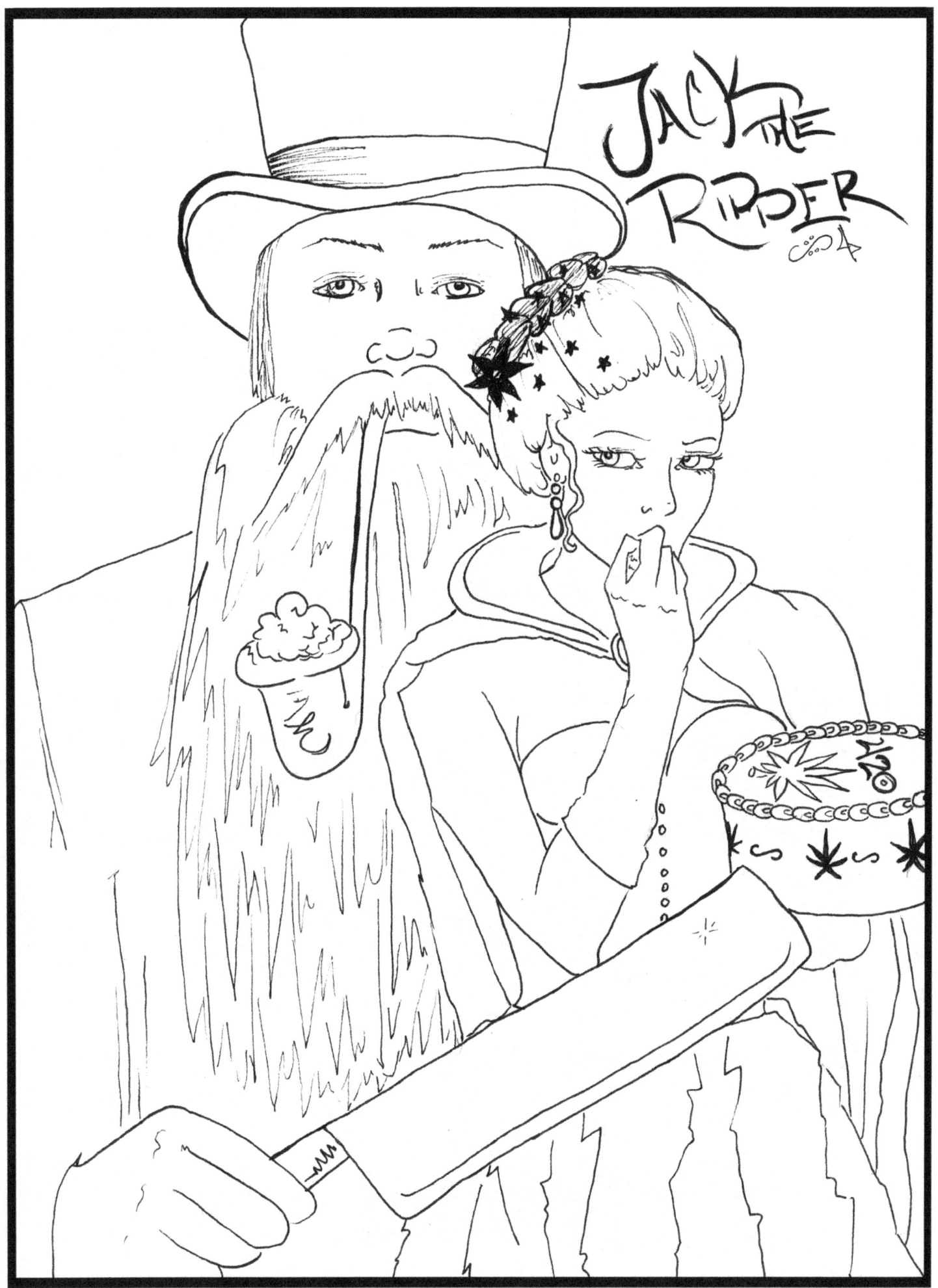

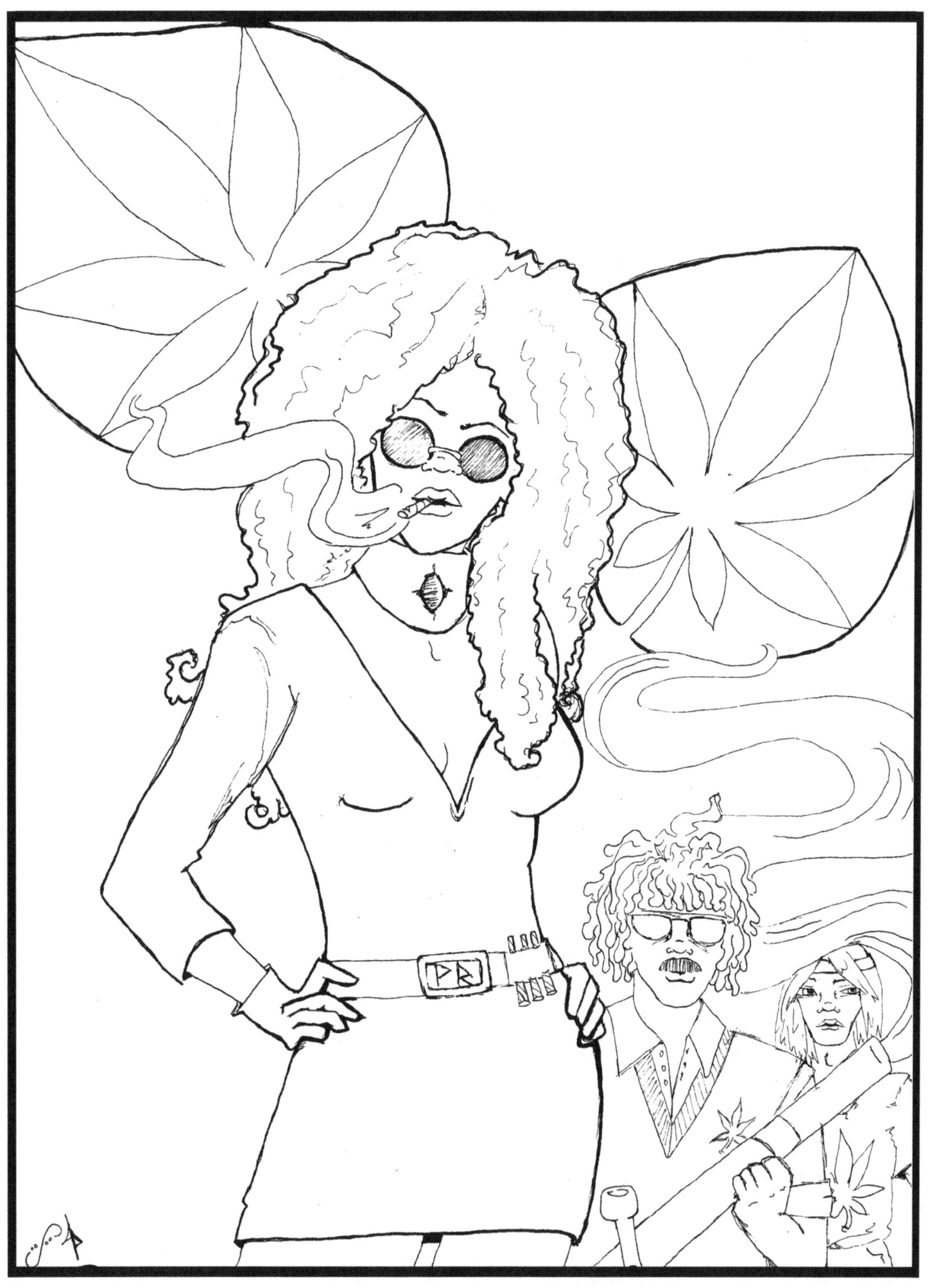

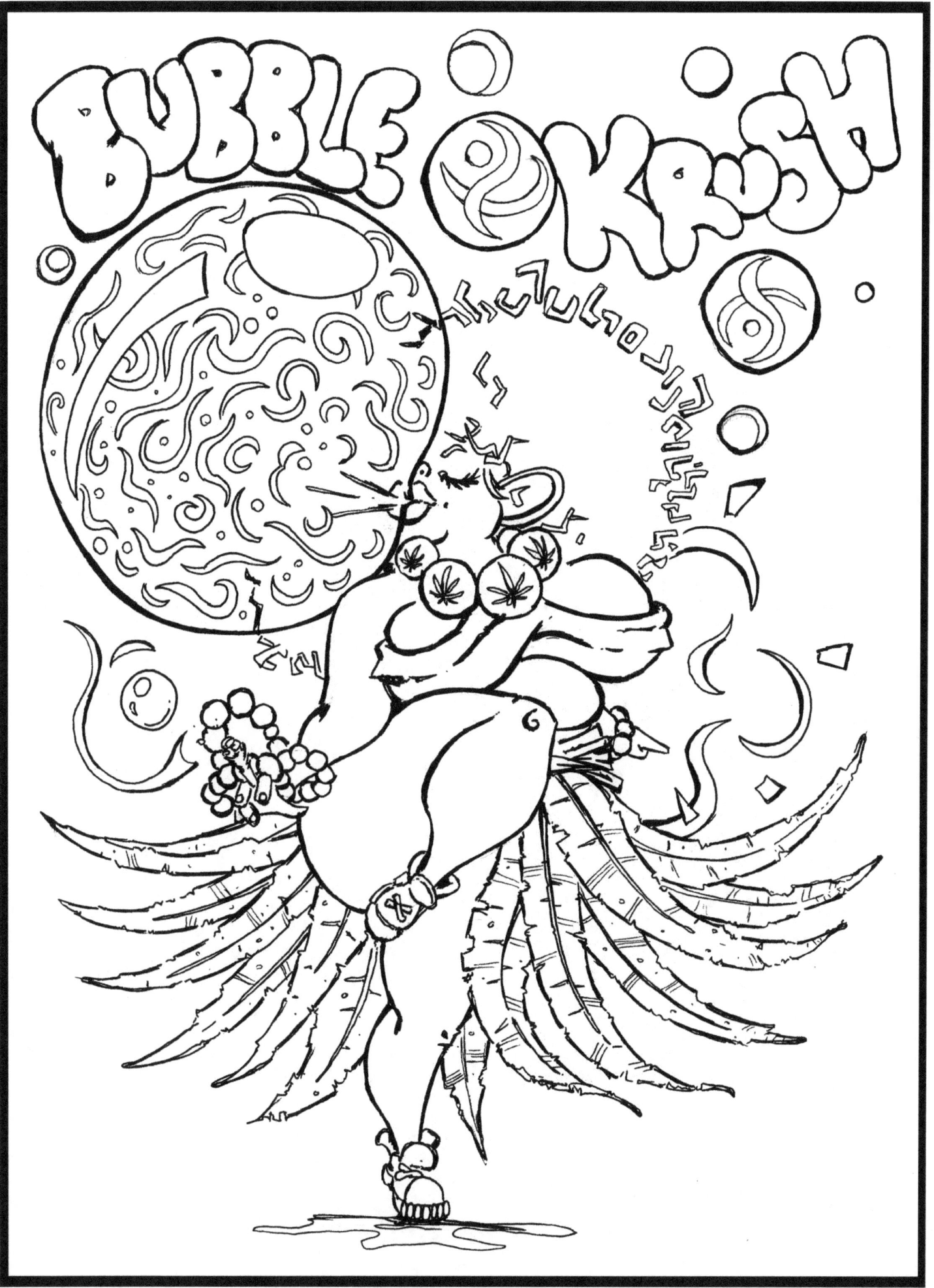

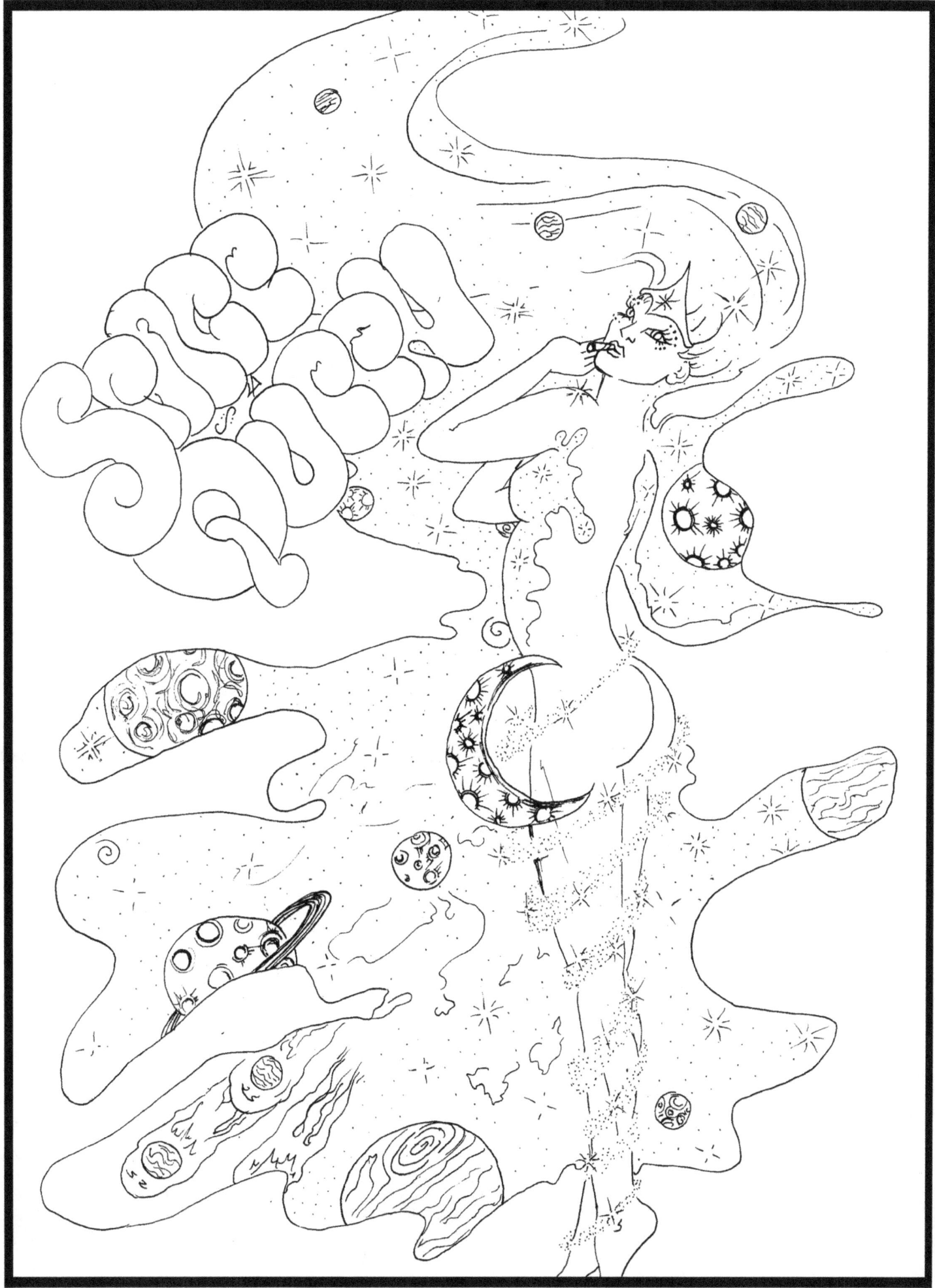

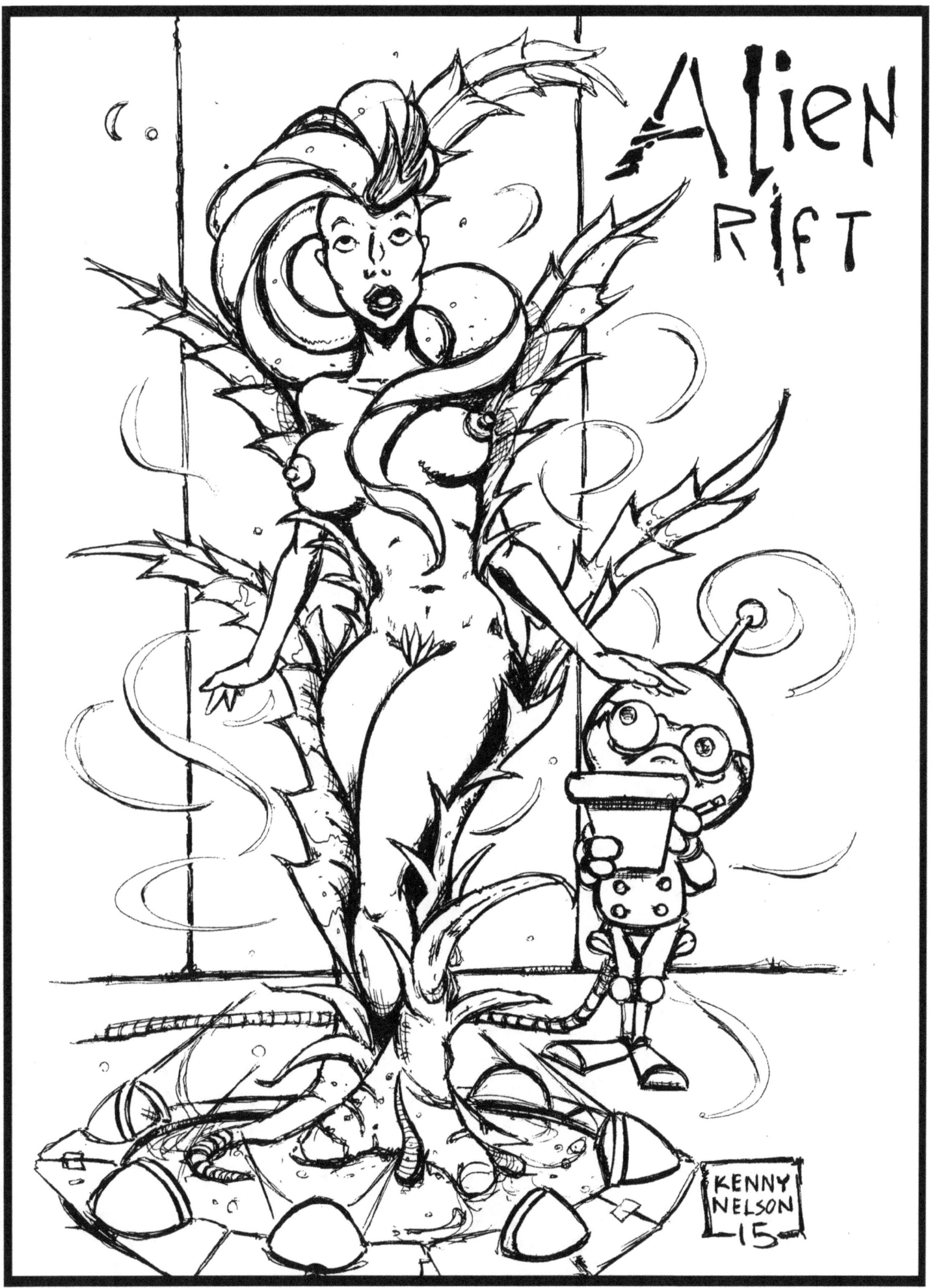

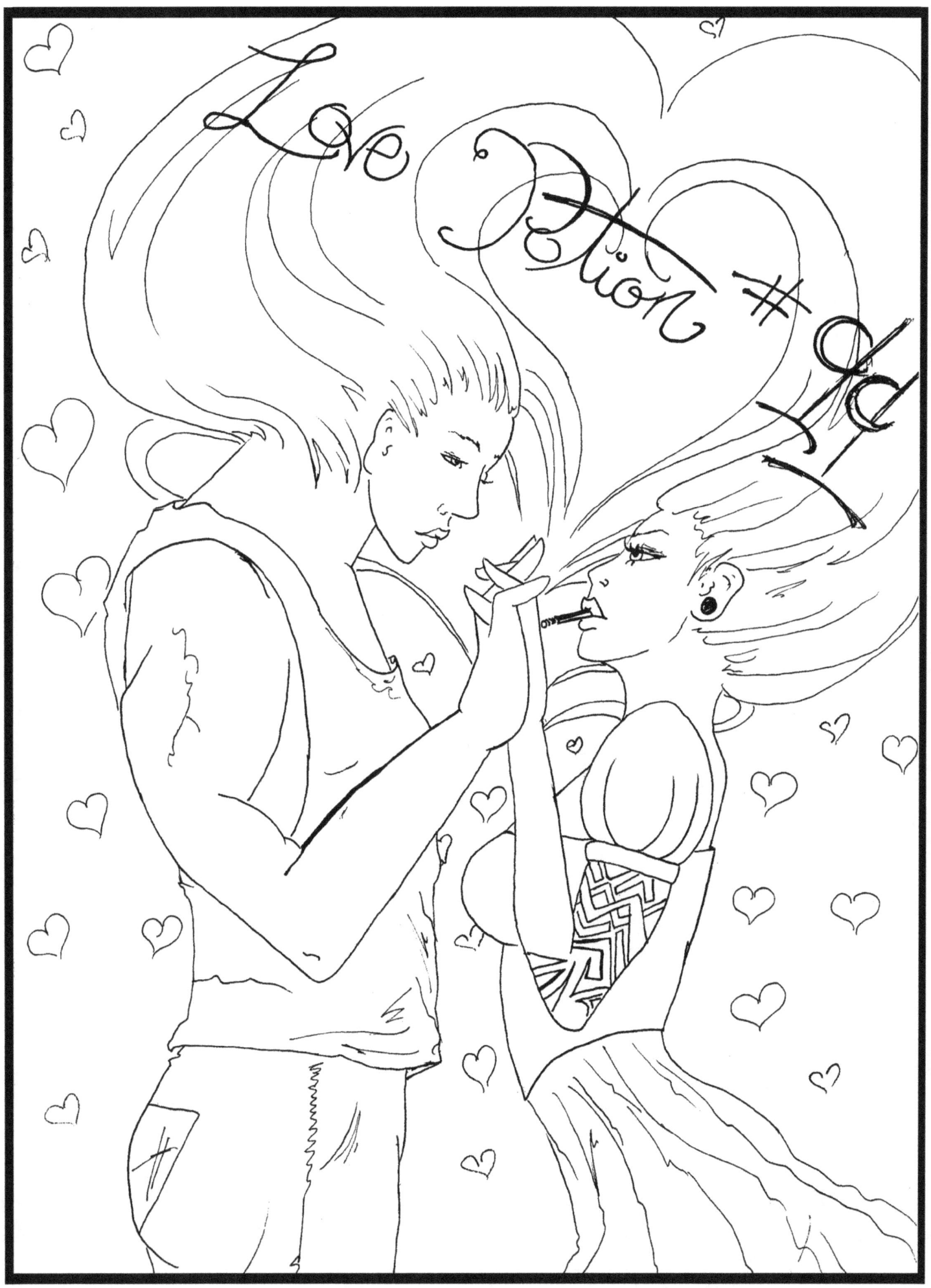

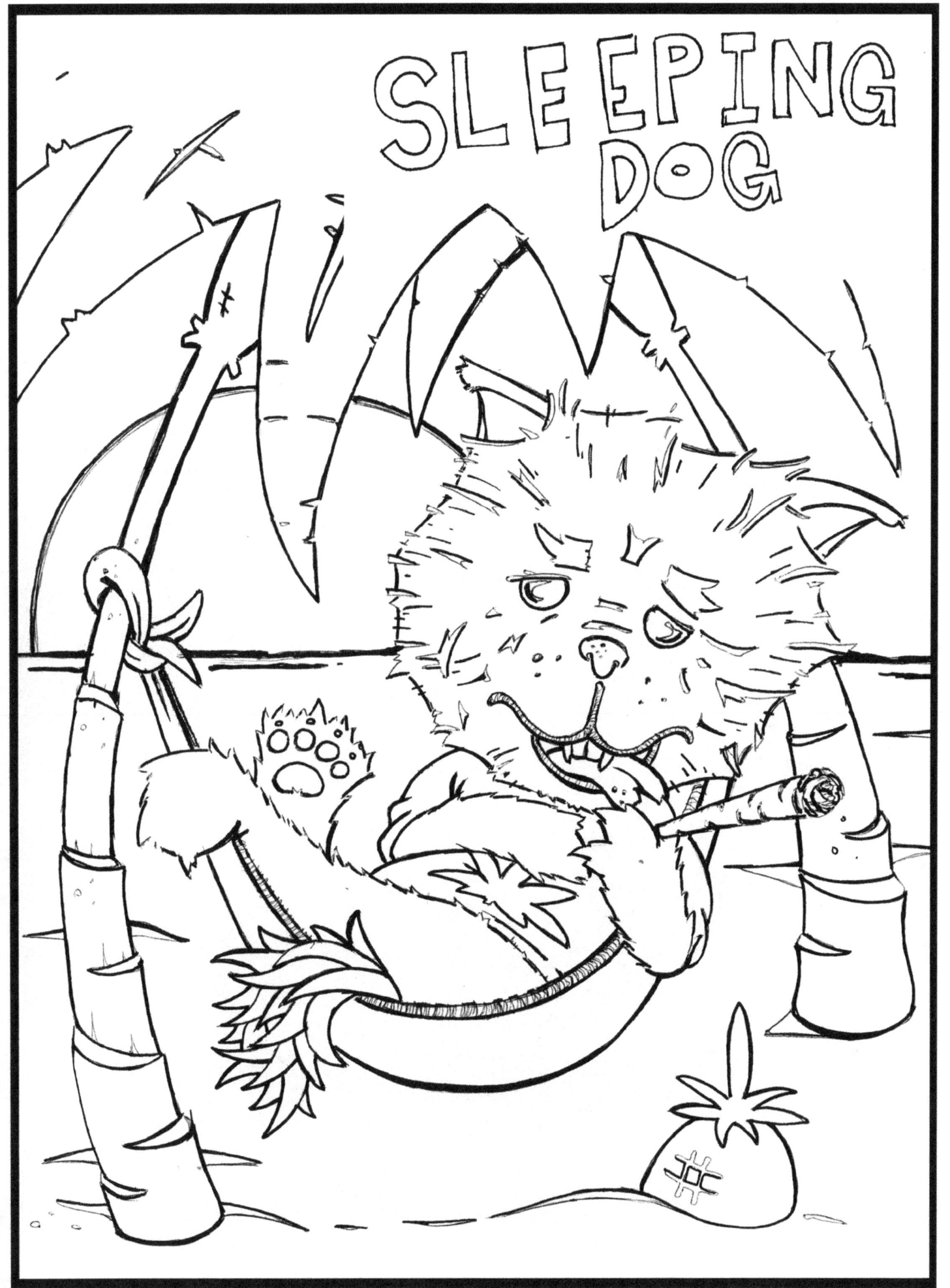

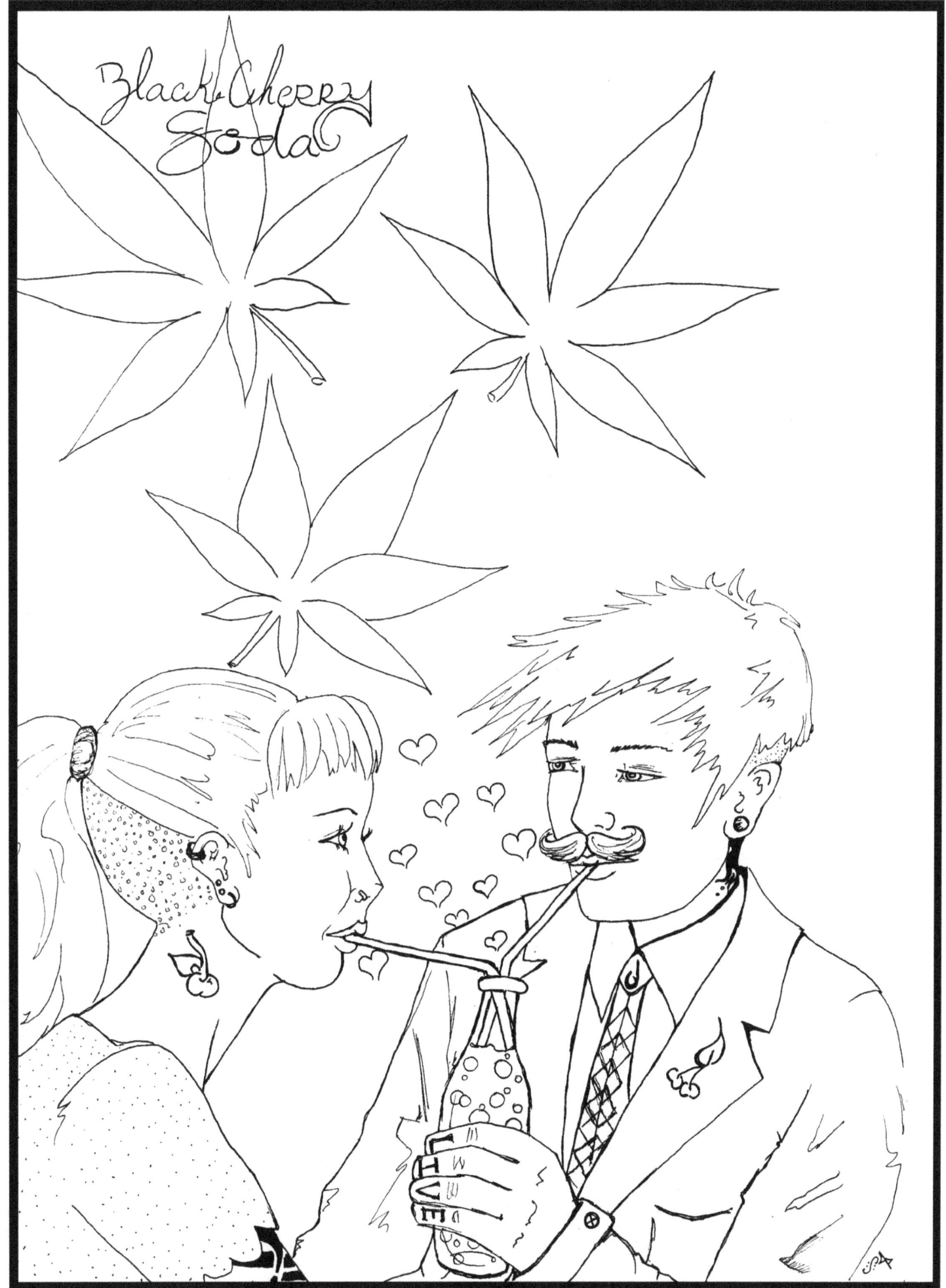

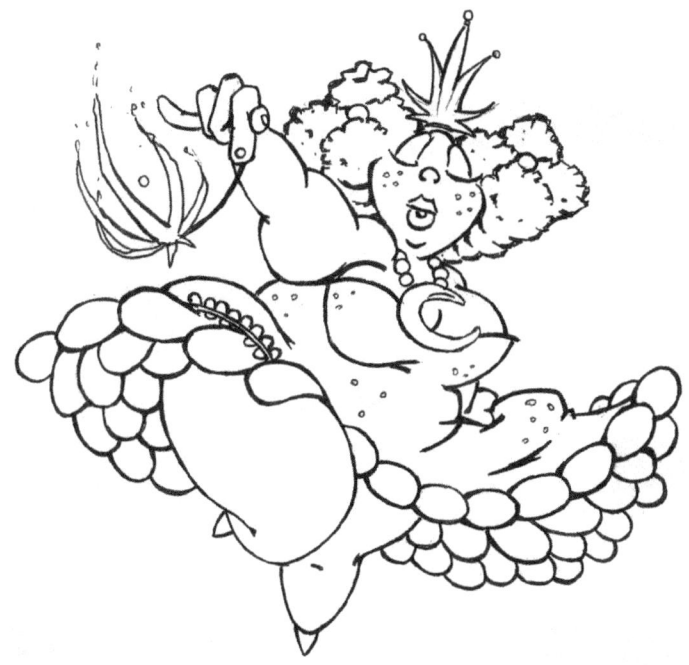

leaf #1
Strawberry Cough
Sativa
Strawberry Fields+Haze

leaf #2
Blue Dream
Hybrid
Blueberry+Haze

leaf #3
Critical Hog
Indica
Critical Mass+Hog

leaf #4
Qrazy Train
Hybrid
Trainwreck+Trinity
+Purple Urkle+Space Queen

leaf #5
Hempstar
Sativa
Skunk+Oasis+Haze

leaf #6
Ace of Spades
Indica
Jack the Ripper
+Black Cherry Soda

leaf #7
Chemdawg
Hybrid
Nepalese+Thai

leaf #8
Girl Scout Cookies
Hybrid
Durban Poison+Og Kush

leaf #9
Dream Queen
Hybrid
Blue Dream+Space Queen

leaf #10
Blue Bubba
Indica
Blue God+Bubba Kush

leaf #11
Dragon's Breath
Hybrid
Hawgsbreath+619 master kush
+Alien abduction

leaf #12
Wizard's Potion
Hybrid
Widow G 13+ SFV Og+Bullrider

leaf #13
Black Cauldron
Indica
Merlot Og+Wizards Potion
+ Merlot V

leaf #14
Jack the Ripper
Sativa
Jack's Cleaners+Space Queen

leaf #15
Private Reserve
Indica
OG#18

leaf #16
Bubble Krush
Hybrid
parents unknown

leaf #17
Space Queen
Hybrid
Romulan+Cinderella 99

leaf #18
Alien Rift
Indica
Alien Abduction+Alien
+ Dawg (Ether)+ Alien go

leaf #19
Love Potion 99
Sativa
parents unknown

leaf #20
Sleeping Dog
Indica
parents unknown

leaf #21
Black Cherry Soda
Hybrid
Airborne G13 X Ortega+C99
+Blackberry+Cherry Ak-4